BEYOND CUSTOMER SERVICE
Keeping Customers for Life

Richard F. Gerson, Ph.D.

A FIFTY-MINUTE™ SERIES BOOK

CRISP PUBLICATIONS, INC.
Menlo Park, California

FLEX TRAINING LTD
9-15 HITCHIN STREET
BALDOCK
HERTS. SG7 6AL
TEL: 01462 895544
FAX: 01462 892417

BEYOND CUSTOMER SERVICE
Keeping Customers for Life

Richard F. Gerson, Ph.D.

CREDITS:
Editor: **Kay Kepler**
Designer: **Carol Harris**
Typesetting: **ExecuStaff**
Cover Design: **Carol Harris**
Artwork: **Ralph Mapson**

Copyright © 1992 Crisp Publications, Inc.
Printed in the United States of America

English language Crisp books are distributed worldwide. Our major international distributors include:

CANADA: Reid Publishing Ltd., Box 69559-109 Thomas St., Oakville, Ontario, Canada L6J 7R4. TEL: (416) 842-4428, FAX: (416) 842-9327

Raincoast Books Distribution Ltd., 112 East 3rd Avenue, Vancouver, British Columbia, Canada V5T 1C8. TEL: (604) 873-6581, FAX: (604) 874-2711.

AUSTRALIA: Career Builders, P. O. Box 1051, Springwood, Brisbane, Queensland, Australia, 4127. TEL: 841-1061, FAX: 841-1580

NEW ZEALAND: Career Builders, P. O. Box 571, Manurewa, Auckland, New Zealand. TEL: 266-5276, FAX: 266-4152

JAPAN: Phoenix Associates Co., Mizuho Bldg. 2-12-2, Kami Osaki, Shinagawa-Ku, Tokyo 141, Japan. TEL: 3-443-7231, FAX: 3-443-7640

Selected Crisp titles are also available in other languages. Contact International Rights Manager Suzanne Kelly at (415) 323-6100 for more information.

Library of Congress Catalog Card Number 91-72653
Gerson, Richard F.
BEYOND CUSTOMER SERVICE
ISBN 1-56052-115-5

This book is printed on recyclable paper with soy ink.

ABOUT THE BOOK

Beyond Customer Service is a very useful resource for both small and large business owners—in fact, for everyone who wants to compete in today's marketplace. With so many businesses offering similar products and services, one of the only ways left to compete is to exceed traditional customer service. This book will tell you how to extend your customer service program into a customer retention program.

Each chapter of *Beyond Customer Service* is a stand-alone unit that explains how to retain your customers for life. Read each chapter entirely, then go back to the particular sections that will help you develop your customer retention program. Remember to use the retention and service techniques as marketing tools to maintain your competitive edge.

Do not rush through this book. Read everything carefully. Take notes. Think about your customer service program, its policies and procedures, and how you can improve the entire system. Customer service is necessary for success in today's business environment. So is customer satisfaction. However, continued success is based on long-term customer retention. This book will provide you with the methods and tactics to keep your customers for life.

ABOUT THE AUTHOR

Richard F. Gerson, Ph.D. is president of Gerson Goodson, Inc., a marketing consulting and management training firm serving small businesses, entrepreneurs, Fortune 500 companies and other consultants. Dr. Gerson's marketing consultations have helped numerous businesses get started and be successful and he has helped several companies bring new products to market. He has also developed a number of unique training programs in the areas of marketing, customer service, communication, team building and personal training for peak performance. This is his second book with Crisp Publications.

Dr. Gerson can be reached by writing or calling:

Richard F. Gerson, Ph.D.
Gerson Goodson, Inc.
P.O. Box 1534
Safety Harbor, Florida 34695
(813) 726-7619

CONTENTS

Dedication:

This book is dedicated to my wife Robbie and our sons Michael and Mitchell, who continue to teach me the true meaning of satisfaction in life. Thank you all.

P A R T

I

Customer Service
and Beyond

DEVELOPING SUPERIOR CUSTOMER SERVICE PROGRAMS

In today's volatile economy, providing excellent customer service can be the critical difference in your company's success.

Customer service does not only mean producing high quality products, although product quality is an important part of customer service. People don't tolerate shoddy goods—they return them and shop somewhere else. First you must sell customers quality products to win them over. Then you must provide superior customer service to keep them.

Customer service involves all the activities your business and your employees conduct or perform to satisfy customers. This means more than just handling complaints, providing refunds or exchanges on returns, and smiling at customers. Customer service also means going out of your way for the customer, doing everything possible to satisfy the customer and making decisions that benefit the customer even at the expense of your company.

THE IMPORTANCE OF CUSTOMER SERVICE

Recall how you felt the last time you had poor service, either at a restaurant, an airport ticket counter or a retail store. In the space provided, describe the situation, what was said, how you felt, what was done and your expectations about purchasing from that provider again. If you decided never to shop there again, what do you think it cost that company not to satisfy you and keep you as a customer?

_____

_____

_____

THE COST OF POOR CUSTOMER SERVICE

Customer service pays, it does not cost. It pays in many ways, the first of which is long-term customer retention. Many businesses understand the cost of acquiring a customer, but they don't understand the cost of losing one. In fact, it costs five to six times more to acquire a customer than it does to do business with a current or former customer.

Figure out how much it costs to lose a customer. The formula is based on information from the U.S. Office of Consumer Affairs. You need to know three figures to complete the formula: your annual revenues, the number of customers you have and your cost of acquiring and keeping them, including marketing, sales, advertising, promotions, discounts, etc. You can use dollar amounts or the percentage of sales to help you determine the cost of poor service.

DEVELOPING SUPERIOR CUSTOMER SERVICE PROGRAMS (continued)

WHAT YOU LOSE

Let us assume that your hypothetical business has revenues of $10 million a year from 2,500 customers. We will also assume that the cost of sales is 66% of revenue, or $6.6 million. Now, plug these figures into the formula on page 5 and see what poor customer service really costs your company.

Take the total number of customers, multiply it by 25% to get your number of dissatisfied customers. Then multiply that result by 70%, which is an estimate of the number of dissatisfied customers who will stop doing business with you. Divide total annual revenues by the number of customers to get the average revenue of one customer, then multiply this by the number who switched, and you get the cost of losing your customers.

Next, calculate your lost opportunity revenue by assuming each dissatisfied customer will tell 10 people. Assume that 2% of these will buy elsewhere. Multiply this number by the average revenue per customer and you get your potential lost revenue.

To determine your customer acquisition and replacement costs, multiply your total annual revenues by 66%, and divide that by your total number of customers to get your average cost per customer. Multiply this result by five to get your replacement cost per customer.

Now, add up all your results to get your total cost of poor service. Multiply that figure by 10 to determine the costs of poor service over a 10-year period, considered to be the customer's lifetime for doing business with you.

No business of any size can afford to lose and seek customers continuously. These results should motivate you to improve your customer service programs so that they become customer retention programs.

THE COST OF POOR SERVICE

Lost Customer Revenue

A.	Annual revenue	$ 10,000,000
B.	Total number of customers	2,500
C.	Percentage of dissatisfied customers	× .25
D.	Number of dissatisfied customers (C × B)	= 625
E.	Percentage of dissatisfied customers who are likely to switch	× .70
F.	Number of dissatisfied customers who will switch	= 437.5
G.	Average revenue per customer (A ÷ B)	$ 4,000
H.	Revenue lost through poor service (F × G)	$ (1,750,000)

Lost Opportunity Revenue

I.	Number of other people dissatisfied customers tell (F × 10)	4,375
J.	Number of potential customers who buy elsewhere due to negative word of mouth (assume one in 50 tell, therefore 1 × .02)	87.5
K.	Potential lost revenue (J × G)	$ (350,000)

Customer Replacement Costs

L.	Customer acquisition costs (66% × A)	$ 6,600,000
M.	Average cost per customer (L ÷ B)	2,640
N.	Replacement cost for lost customers (M × 5)	$ (13,200)

Total Costs

O.	Total annual cost (H + K + N)	$ (2,113,200)
P.	Total cost over customer's lifetime of doing business for 10 years (O × 10)	$(21,132,000)

As you can see from this frightening example, our hypothetical company will lose more than $2 million a year due to poor service and customer retention. Now fill in the same chart for your company. Your results will probably motivate you to improve your customer service and retention efforts.

WHAT YOU LOSE (continued)

THE COST OF POOR SERVICE

Fill in this chart for your own company.

Lost Customer Revenue

A. Annual revenue .... $ _____

B. Total number of customers .... _____

C. Percentage of dissatisfied customers .... × .25

D. Number of dissatisfied customers (C × B) .... = _____

E. Percentage of dissatisfied customers who are likely to switch × .70

F. Number of dissatisfied customers who will switch .... = _____

G. Average revenue per customer (A ÷ B) .... $ _____

H. Revenue lost through poor service (F × G) .... $ _____

Lost Opportunity Revenue

I. Number of other people dissatisfied customers tell (F × 10) .. _____

J. Number of potential customers who buy elsewhere due to negative word of mouth (assume one in 50 tell, therefore 1 × .02) .... _____

K. Potential lost revenue (J × G) .... $ _____

Customer Replacement Costs

L. Customer acquisition costs (___% × A) .... $ _____

M. Average cost per customer (L ÷ B) .... $ _____

N. Replacement cost for lost customers (M × 5) .... $ _____

Total Costs

O. Total annual cost (H + K + N) .... $ _____

P. Total cost over customer's lifetime of doing business for 10 years (O × 10) .... $ _____

CUSTOMER SERVICE: ONE, TWO, THREE

Poor customer service is expensive. Good customer service is invaluable, and you can achieve it in your company. First, you must realize that service is both a marketing and a management tool for your business. It enhances marketing because it motivates customers to spread the good word about your service and business to others. Remember, the least expensive way to acquire new customers is through word of mouth. Good service makes management easier because everybody is committed to satisfying the customer. The results will be increased productivity and profits simply because management and employees are working to achieve the same goal.

Next, develop a customer service system for your company that is easy for your customers to use.*

Last, design and implement customer retention programs that will maintain customer loyalty, thereby increasing the probability that your customers will refer new buyers to your business. Also, remember to use these retention programs as both primary and supplementary marketing tools.

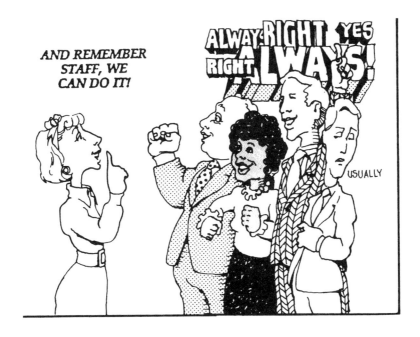

*See Martin, William, *Quality Customer Service,* and Scott, Dru, *Customer Satisfaction: The Second Half of Your Job,* both by Crisp Publications.

SEVEN STEPS TO A SUCCESSFUL CUSTOMER SERVICE SYSTEM

Developing a successful customer service system can be one of the most rewarding goals you achieve for your company. Like most goals, it requires planning and work. Following these seven steps will place you ahead of your competition and start you on your way to successful customer retention.

STEP 1. TOTAL MANAGEMENT COMMITMENT

Customer service programs cannot succeed within a company unless top management is committed to the concept. It is up to the president, CEO or owner to develop a clear and concise service vision for the company. Then management must communicate that vision, as the company's service mission statement, to all the employees. Use the space below to write your own vision or mission statement for customer service and retention.

_____

_____

_____

_____

STEP 2. GET TO KNOW YOUR CUSTOMERS

Not only must you get to know your customers intimately, you must also understand them totally. You need to know what they like about you, what they dislike, what they want changed, how they want it changed, what needs they have, what their expectations are, what motivates them to buy, what satisfies them and what you must continue to do to maintain their loyalty. The most effective way to get this information is simply to ask your customers.

Once you start to know your customers, you must continue to learn about them. Their needs change on a regular—even daily—basis and you must keep up with them. Make it a policy that you will call your customers at least once a month to find out how they are doing and what they need. While this shows them you are interested in providing good customer service, it also helps you develop effective customer retention programs because it tells your customers you are interested in them as people.

STEP 3. DEVELOP STANDARDS OF SERVICE QUALITY PERFORMANCE

Customer service is not as intangible a concept as you may think. Each business has specific business practices that could be improved. For example, how many times does the phone ring before someone answers it? How many call transfers does it take to find someone to answer the customer's question? How long does it take to process an order or ship a replacement? When standards are set for ordinary business practices, you can be assured of superior performance by your employees. Remember, what gets measured gets done.

STEP 4. HIRE, TRAIN AND COMPENSATE GOOD STAFF

Good customer service and effective customer retention programs can be provided only by competent, qualified people. Your service is only as professional as the people who deliver it. If you want your business to be good to people, hire good people.

Then train them to provide the ultimate in customer service and retention. Be sure they understand what your company's standards of service are. Compensate them well because they are the primary contact your customers have with your company and the reason people will continue to do business with you. Also, these people *are* your company in the eyes and minds of the customers.

Give your staff the authority to make decisions on the spot to satisfy customers. Remember that serving and retaining customers is one of the hardest jobs in a company. If people have that responsibility, they must also have the authority to decide what they can do for a customer.

STEP 5. REWARD SERVICE ACCOMPLISHMENTS

Always recognize, reward and reinforce superior performances. Provide financial and psychological rewards and incentives for your people. Recognize the small wins and accomplishments the same way you would applaud and dramatize the major wins.

You must also reward your customers for good customer behavior. They appreciate recognition the same way your employees do. Recognizing your customers will go a long way toward retaining them and having them refer new people to you.

SEVEN STEPS TO A SUCCESSFUL CUSTOMER SERVICE SYSTEM (continued)

STEP 6. STAY CLOSE TO YOUR CUSTOMERS

Always stay in touch with your customers. Conduct continuous research to learn from them. Ask them questions right after they make a purchase, send them surveys in the mail, run contests that require participation in a survey, hold focus groups to get perceptions and opinions of your business, call them on the telephone, develop a customer council to advise you on their needs, and do anything else you must do to stay close to your customers. Most important of all, LISTEN to them.

Your relationship with the customer actually begins after the purchase is made. This is when you must activate your retention programs, and this is when the customer will get to see how much you really care. Arrange all customer interactions so they are win-win situations for both of you. The result will be more loyal customers.

STEP 7. WORK TOWARD CONTINUOUS IMPROVEMENT

Even though you have designed friendly and accessible customer service systems, hired and trained the best people and gone out of your way to learn about and satisfy your customers needs, you must remember that no system, business or program is perfect. Therefore, you must continuously work to improve your customer service and retention programs.

Your attempts at continuous improvement will be viewed positively by the customers and your employees. They will see that you are trying to become even better than you already are. And when you become better, your service to them will also be better. The result is more satisfied customers, more business for you and your staff, and greater profits.

Customer service pays, it does not cost. You must constantly work to provide the best service at all times. Your only goal for being in business should be to satisfy your customers. Once this is done, the growth, expansion and profits will take care of themselves. Follow these seven steps to implementing a customer service system, and you will find that it will be easy for you to go beyond customer service.

KEEPING YOUR CUSTOMERS

Customers today are better educated than ever before. They are more careful about their purchases and the dollars they spend. They want value for their money. They also want good service and they are willing to pay for it. But who are these customers, and how do you know when they're happy?

STARTLING SERVICE STATISTICS

► Only 4% of customers ever complain. That means your business may never hear from 96% of its customers, and 91% of those just go away because they feel complaining will not do them any good. In fact, complainers are more likely to continue doing business with you than noncomplainers.

► For every complaint your business receives, there are 26 other customers with unresolved complaints or problems, and six of those customers have serious problems. These are people you probably will never hear from. These are also people who can tell you how to make your business better. Get their feedback any way you can.

► Most customers who complain to you (54%–70%) will do business with you again if you resolve their complaint. If they feel you acted quickly and to their satisfaction, then up to 95% of them will do business with you again, and they probably will refer other people to you.

► A dissatisfied customer will tell up to 10 people about it. Approximately 13% of those will tell up to 20 people about their problem. You cannot afford the advertising to overcome this negative word of mouth.

► Happy customers, or customers who have had their complaints resolved, will tell between three and five people about their positive experience. Therefore, you have to satisfy three to four customers for every one that is dissatisfied with you. It is very difficult in any business to work with a 4:1 ratio against you. Customer retention programs will enhance the value of your customer service efforts.

► It costs five to six times more to attract new customers than to keep old ones, even when you have to go back and renew contacts with former customers. Additionally, customer loyalty and the lifetime value of a customer can be worth up to 10 times as much as the price of a single purchase.

STARTLING SERVICE STATISTICS
(continued)

► Businesses that provide superior customer service can charge more, realize greater profits, increase their market share and have customers willingly pay more for their products simply because of the good service. In fact, you can gain an average of 6% a year in market share simply by providing good service: satisfying and keeping your customers.

► The lifetime value of a customer, or the amount of purchases that customer would make over 10 years, is worth more than the cost of returning their purchase price of one item. For example, supermarkets realize up to $5,000 a year from one family. That means $50,000 over 10 years. Is it worth it for them to provide refunds when the customer returns a purchase? Is it worth it to you to have the good will and positive word of mouth this type of retention service will bring you?

► Customer service is governed by the rule of 10s. If it costs $10,000 to get a new customer, it takes only 10 seconds to lose one, and 10 years to get over it or for the problem to be resolved. You must work to keep your customers.

► Customers stop doing business with you because:

- 1% die

- 3% move away

- 5% seek alternatives or develop other business relationships

- 9% begin doing business with the competition

- 14% are dissatisfied with the product or service

- 68% are upset with the treatment they have received

If you look at these percentages, you actually have some control over 96% of the reasons customers stop doing business with you.

WHAT CAN YOU DO?

> Write down the reasons you think people might stop doing business with you. Obviously poor service is one of them, but what other reasons come to mind? After you write down a reason, describe what you would do to correct the problem.
>
> *Reasons to Stop Doing Business*   *Solutions*
>
> _____
>
> _____
>
> _____
>
> _____
>
> _____
>
> _____
>
> _____
>
> _____
>
> _____
>
> _____
>
> _____
>
> _____
>
> _____
>
> _____
>
> _____
>
> _____

These statistics and the chart that helped you calculate the cost of losing customers emphasize the importance of customer retention programs. It is no longer enough to say your company provides good customer service. Nor is it enough to train and empower your people to offer those service behaviors that will satisfy the customers. It is only through customer retention programs that you will be able to maintain your market share and competitive edge, keep your current customers, and remain profitable.

REASONS FOR POOR SERVICE

Ask any consumer why companies give poor service, and they'll tell you. Some problems are common to many businesses. How many of them apply to your organization? Does your company have any unique service problems?

- Uncaring employees

- Poor employee training

- Negative attitudes of employees toward customers

- Differences in perception between what businesses think customers want and what customers actually want

- Differences in perception between the product or service businesses think they provide and what customers think they receive

- Differences in perception between the way businesses think customers want to be treated and the way customers really want to be treated, or are actually treated

- No customer service philosophy within the company

- Poor handling and resolution of complaints

- Employees are not empowered to provide good service, take responsibility, and make decisions that will satisfy the customer

- Poor treatment of employees as customers

Remember that people are loyal to a business because they feel they are treated well, they receive good value for their money, and they are psychologically or physically attached to the business. You must do everything possible to make certain that your customers do not want to switch to your competitors.

Shoppers are price conscious. They often will switch brands or business suppliers simply because one provides a price advantage over the other. You can prevent this by providing superior customer service and employing customer retention strategies. Make it hard for them to leave you. Establish a personal relationship with your customers so that you maintain their loyalty and they continue to do business with you.

Never take a customer for granted. Be grateful they have decided to do business with you and not a competitor. Work as hard as you possibly can to deliver more than they expect, and you will have gone a long way toward retaining your customers.

P A R T

II

Customer Retention

DEVELOPING CUSTOMER RETENTION PROGRAMS

Customer service does not exist in a vacuum and neither do customer retention programs. You need an overall structure or guiding focus to make them work. Consider marketing as that guiding principle, and create all your customer retention programs under your marketing umbrella. This will enable you to track and evaluate your efforts. Once you set up the programs within the marketing plan, you can use customer service as an effective yet inexpensive marketing tool.*

Most think of customer service as something they do after the fact. They view the process more as a complaint-handling system than a marketing technique. Complaint handling is only one small part of customer service. You must make the decision now to develop superior customer service and retention programs that are proactive, rather than reactive.

PROACTIVE VS REACTIVE EFFORTS

Customer service has two sides. Reactive customer service comes after the fact—after a customer has had a problem, a complaint, is dissatisfied or has had to bring something to the attention of a business. Proactive service begins even before the customer walks in the door. Your business is already prepared to do everything possible to satisfy and keep the customer.

*See R.F. Gerson, *Writing and Implementing a Marketing Plan,* by Crisp Publications.

DEVELOPING CUSTOMER RETENTION PROGRAMS (continued)

One of the best examples of proactive service is making the buying experience as easy as possible for the customer. Speed up the purchase process, decrease waiting times (people hate to wait), make your business a nice place to be. Many businesses, especially service businesses, do not have a tangible item to sell. Therefore, the office, the appearance of the facility or the people, is the only tangible item the customer sees. You must make it pleasant and appealing. People will continue to do business with you because they like the way you look and this makes them feel comfortable.

Proactive service and retention does wonders for a company's bottom line. Add to this some other retention-getters, such as thanking customers for coming in, thanking them for shopping even when they do not buy, and offering them additional information so that they can make a better purchase decision. You will find they will keep coming back to you simply because you created a pleasant atmosphere, made it a nice place for them to shop and made it easy for them to buy.

Think of some ways you can be proactive in the service you provide to customers. What can you do for them before it needs doing so that they will want to continue to do business with you? Write down ideas, then try to implement one idea a week. You will be pleasantly surprised at the results.

_____

_____

_____

_____

_____

_____

_____

_____

_____

_____

INTERNAL *AND* EXTERNAL SERVICE

Everybody thinks of customer service as something you do to or for those people who buy from you. Another group of customers also deserves good service, and that group is your staff. Everyone who works for you or with you is also a customer. You must provide your employees with the same type of superior service and retention efforts as you do the buyers of your products. You cannot expect employees to provide excellent customer service if they are not treated well by their employer.

Ask yourself another question and write the answer below. Then check it with the explanation that follows.

Whom do you work for?

_____

Your simplest, one-line answer should have been the customer. If you are an employer or a business owner, you work for the buying customer and your employee customer. If you are an employee, you work for the buying customer and the other people who depend upon your work. Basically, if you are not directly serving the buying customer, you better be working for someone who is.

EMPLOYEES AS CUSTOMERS

Employees are customers, too. So are their families and your stockholders. You must work to serve and retain them. You already know the cost of poor service to a buying customer. Now, what does poor service to an employee cost? You must include:

- Lost salaries paid to employees who have left the company

- Recruitment and hiring costs of new employees

- Training costs for new employees

- Turnover as a percentage of sales and profits

- Negative image as a company with high turnover

Do you have any additional factors that may be figured into the cost of not retaining your employees?

INTERNAL *AND* EXTERNAL SERVICE
(continued)

Employee retention is simply a function of superior internal customer service. Recruit, hire and train the best people with the best people attitudes. Then, empower them to make decisions. Give them authority to go with the responsibility they have of serving the customer. Recognize and reward their accomplishments and achievements. Treat them as you would your best customers. You will see tremendous results, such as lower recruiting and replacement costs, because more people will stay with you longer. These people will refer people to work for you so you do not have to spend money on recruiting. Above all, remember that if you serve your employees well, they will serve you and your customers well.

RETENTION THROUGH VALUE CHAINS

A chain is only as strong as its weakest link. As a business, you have suppliers and final customers, with employees in between. This is your value chain. Set it up so that every link is strong.

Treat your suppliers right. Order what you know they can deliver. Expect delivery within a reasonable amount of time. Pay your bills to them on time or early. Reward their loyalty with more business. Create enhanced value for them so they will continue to do business with you.

Treat your employees right. They deserve it and your customers deserve it.

Treat your customers right. Listen to them. Find out what they need, want and expect. Then give them everything and more. Exceed their expectations. Put more value in the chain. Let them know who your suppliers are and how well you treat your employees. This will make them comfortable and secure with you, and they will continue to do business with you.

VALUE CHAIN

Draw your own value chain below. A basic, three-link chain has been provided for you. Follow it or create your own. Then list the actions you can take to add more value to your customer interactions.

ACTIONS:

_____

_____

_____

_____

VALUE-ADDED SERVICE

Drawing the value chain is the first step to providing value-added service. Value-added service means giving the customers more than they expect. Sometimes you can charge more for value-added service, because customers will pay the added price just to receive the quality service.

An example of value-added service is the concept of the "baker's dozen": you pay for 12 items and receive 13. Some companies have extended this idea to give you 14 or 15 items for the price of 12. This is their attempt to compete by providing value-added service.

Perhaps an employee decides that customer satisfaction is more important than company policy. For example, companies have policies stating that refunds or exchanges will be made only with the original sales receipt and carton before 30 days. If you ever brought something back on the 31st day, or without the receipt, and had a company representative accept it from you, you received value-added service.

By doing this, the representative ensures that you will be a satisfied customer and that you will continue to do business with their company. On the other hand, if you brought the item back, were rudely treated and told that the policy forbids late exchanges, how would you feel? Would you do business with them again? Probably not.

To see how well you're doing with your customers, check with your competition to see what they are doing with value-added service enhancements. If they are doing something you like, adapt it and make it work for your company.

Use the chart below to help you.

Competitor's Service Policy	What I Like	How I Will Adapt It

Now let's see how you can introduce value-added enhancements to your business.

Fill in the chart below to help you provide value-added service as a customer retention tool. Write your current customer service programs in the left column and the ways you will add value to them in the right column. When you have completed the chart, describe how these new value-added service enhancements will help your business.

COMPANY POLICIES	VALUE-ADDED ENHANCEMENTS
1.	
2.	
3.	
4.	
5.	
6.	
7.	
8.	
9.	
10.	

These enhancements will help my business by:

1. _____

2. _____

3. _____

4. _____

5. _____

SERVICE ENHANCEMENTS

Value-added service can be expanded to include service enhancements, which are basically the services you already offer with some improvements.

For example, let us assume you are a car dealer who guarantees repair work for six months or the car is repaired again, free. A service enhancement to this policy would be to provide the owner with a loaner car while you work on their car. If it is the second or third time you are trying to fix the same problem, and the fault is yours, you can refund the money for the original repair just because your customer was inconvenienced by bringing the car back again.

Or you could give a free gift with a purchase. This creates the perception that people are getting more for their money. And you know how everyone likes to receive a bargain.

What other types of service enhancements can you provide? Maybe you can offer toll-free telephone numbers, free service calls or replacement parts for products under guarantee or warranty. List your service enhancements and why they would interest your customers. Be very specific when you list the benefits, as these become excellent marketing and advertising messages.

Current Service	Service Enhancement	Benefit

RETENTION THROUGH CUSTOMER SERVICE MARKETING

Your business doesn't have to be on a seesaw of losing customers and seeking new ones. You can go beyond customer service, increase customer retention and enhance your marketing efforts all at the same time. In fact, your customer retention policies double as excellent marketing approaches for your business.

Take the following quiz. Answer each question with a ''yes'' or ''no.'' On a separate sheet of paper, describe why you do or do not perform any of the following activities.

Does your business engage in:

	Yes	No
1. Frequent buyer programs	____	____
2. Frequent referral programs	____	____
3. Thank-you cards	____	____
4. Newsletters/Personal letter	____	____
5. Telephone recalls	____	____
6. Customer reward and recognition programs	____	____
7. Customer special events	____	____
8. Strategic alliances or partnerships	____	____

These 8 ideas are all customer retention policies that are also good marketing strategies for your business. The more ''no'' answers you have, the more programs you will have to develop and implement to retain your customers.

RETENTION THROUGH CUSTOMER SERVICE MARKETING (continued)

1. FREQUENT BUYER PROGRAMS

Frequent buyer programs are similar to the airlines' frequent flyer programs. You are rewarding those customers who buy from you regularly. The rewards do not have to be expensive or lavish, they just have to show the customer you appreciate their business. Be sure it is easy for all your regular customers to benefit from this program.

Consider a retail store that punches a card every time you buy something. After your tenth or twelfth purchase, you get something for free or at a significant discount. This policy encourages you to go back to shop there because you will receive a special reward when you meet a specific criterion. Repeat purchase cards are an excellent way to retain customers, and they are an excellent marketing tool, as well.

2. FREQUENT REFERRAL PROGRAMS

If your business depends on referrals, you should reward the people making referrals to you. Your rewards will also reinforce their behavior, thereby creating a positive cycle and a mutually beneficial relationship.

The best way to use a frequent referral reward program is to develop it in tiers, or levels. Here are some suggestions for rewards based on the number of referrals from one source. Don't forget to fill in how you would reinforce this behavior. Also, feel free to change the reward recommendation to suit your business or situation.

Number of Referrals	Reward Recommendation	My Reward
1	Thank you card	
2	Telephone call	
3	Flowers	
4	Small gift (under $10)	
5	Gift certificate (dinner for two)	

When the same person refers more than five people, do something special for that person. Then start the referral reward program all over again.

If your customers don't mind having their names visible in your store or office, create a referral thank you bulletin board. Post the names of your current customers who refer new customers to you on this board each month. You can also post the number of referrals they have made. People usually like to see their name written on something, and this will give them the satisfaction of knowing you appreciate their efforts. Also, it may create a healthy competition among your customers to see who can refer more new people to you each month. They benefit because you will reward and reinforce them and you benefit from the new business and positive word of mouth.

Create a new customer welcome bulletin board. List the names of your new customers each month. This is the first step in a proactive customer retention program. When people see that you care enough to put their name up for everyone else to see, they will go out of their way to help you in your business and to remain loyal to you.

3. THANK YOU CARDS

A simple and effective customer retention technique that few businesses exploit, writing a thank you card and sending it to someone who has bought something from you, takes only a little extra effort. Cards are the best postage-stamp marketing investment you can make.

If you do not want to write out a card for every customer that purchases, then have your cards preprinted with a message that shows your appreciation. It is even more effective if you develop part of your customer retention program around a series of these cards.

THANK YOU CARDS

THANK YOU CARDS (continued)

Displayed are samples of preprinted cards that I use for all my customers. You can make them up at your local printer or purchase them from a specialty dealer. The cards are sent out in the order you see them: ''Thank you for your business''; ''Our customers are number 1''; and when the job is completed, ''It was a pleasure working with you.'' When my company receives a referral, we send out the referral thank you card. All this information and the dates the cards are sent are tracked through our customer database.

Front

Inside

e value your business highly and hope to be of service to you many times in the future.

Company Name Here

Front

Inside

We appreciate
your business and thank
you for the opportunity
of serving you!
You can always count
on our support!

Company Name Here

Front

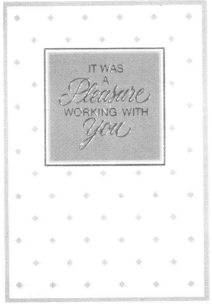

Inside

*H*ope we get the
opportunity to do it again
in the near future.

Company Name Here

Front

Inside

*Y*our confidence in us
is greatly appreciated.

Company Name Here

4. NEWSLETTERS/PERSONAL LETTER

Newsletters are a great way to keep your customers informed of what is going on in your business. You can tell them whatever information you need for them to know. And, because it is coming from you free of charge, they will be only too glad to read it.

One way to keep your customers involved with your business is to promote contests or other activities in the newsletter. Specify that they come to your store or office to win the contest. This is another good time to solidify their loyalty and make sure you retain them as customers.

One variation of the newsletter is a letter of news. Write a personal letter to each customer (using a computerized customer database makes this task very easy) and mention all the items you would have mentioned in a newsletter. Your customers will be pleased that you took the time to write them a personal letter. Here is an example of a one- to two-page letter of news:

SAMPLE—PERSONAL LETTER

Today's Date

Michael Mitchell
Any House
Anytown, USA

Dear Michael Mitchell:

I just wanted to thank you for continuing to do business with us. I also wanted to take this opportunity to tell you about some of the great things that are happening in our business and how they can benefit you. As you know, we have provided both marketing consulting and training services for you in the past year. Your comments indicated you were very satisfied and are interested in working with us again. Here is some exciting news to help you decide on when we can begin these programs.

New Marketing Book Gets Published

I have recently had the honor of having a marketing book published by Crisp Publications. It is called *Writing and Implementing a Marketing Plan.* The book sells for $7.95. It is available to all our marketing consulting clients free of charge. If you participate in one of our marketing workshops, it is given to you as part of the workshop fee. It also reduces the cost of the workshop to you, since now there is no materials charge.

Corporate Videos Being Filmed

Several large corporations have asked us to film their presentations to prospective clients. Our videos are professionally done using state-of-the-art equipment. They can be as long as you need to get your message across. We provide all the necessary services, including script writing, filming, editing, sound, pre- and post-production.

The Last Training Seminar You Will Ever Need

It has taken more than 20 years of research in psychology, human behavior, human relations and communications. Now we have designed a training program that can help you achieve greater personal and professional success, more sales, more friendships, deeper and more meaningful relationships and a better love life. It is called *Success Through Effective Human Relations,* and it teaches you about people's behavioral and interpersonal styles, sensory perceptual communication styles and the basic principles of effective human relations. The program is customized to suit your needs and budget.

I hope this information has been helpful to you. Please feel free to call me at (813) 726-7619 if you have any questions. Or, just stop by to see us to say hello. We appreciate you as our customer, and we look forward to continuing our relationship with you.

Sincerely,

Richard F. Gerson, Ph.D.
President

P.S. Look for my newest book, *Beyond Customer Service,* which will be published in early 1992 by Crisp Publications. It provides you with many ideas on how to get and keep customers for life.

5. TELEPHONE RECALLS

Telephone recalls work well in any type of business. If you are in a service business where customers need to make appointments, you can call them a day in advance to remind them of the appointment. Or, if they have not been in to see you in some time, you can call them to see how they are doing and to inform them of a reason to come in now to do business with you.

If your business is retail, you can personally call customers and invite them into a special sale. This is often done by department stores who send mailers to their credit card holders inviting them to a sale before the general public is invited. If this makes you feel special, think how much more special you will feel when someone calls you personally.

When you are not able to make all the calls personally, write out a basic script for the caller. You want your message of caring for the customer to come across loud and clear.

When your customers call you, treat them with courtesy. Answer the phone in the following way: ''Good (morning, afternoon), (company name), this is (your name). How may I help you?''

Never put a caller on hold for more than 30 seconds without coming back and telling them what the delay is. People hate to wait, and they will hang up and take their business elsewhere. If your customers complain that they cannot get through to you on the telephone, it may be time to install more telephone lines.

Some businesses use the telephone as their life's blood. Do not make the mistake of neglecting the telephone as a way to retain your customers. Call them regularly, even if it is just to say hello.

6. CUSTOMER REWARD & RECOGNITION PROGRAMS

Recognizing and rewarding your customers should be a regular business practice. Sending thank you cards tells customers you recognize their importance to your business. Giving them gifts for referrals shows them how much you appreciate their efforts on your behalf. Offering them rewards for making repeat purchases informs them you understand their contribution to your business success. But you can do more to retain customers.

First, recognize every customer that does business with you. Learn and use their names. If you cannot remember someone's name, at least acknowledge that you recognize that person as a regular customer. If someone is a new customer, go out of your way to learn their name and everything you can about them. They will appreciate your interest in them.

Next, make your customers feel important. Many businesses say they do this, but it is just not so. You have to give extra effort to make customers feel important, and once you do, you will keep them for life.

What are some ways you can make them feel important? Try these suggestions:

- Ask them about their family, especially their children or grandchildren.

- Congratulate them on some achievement or a job promotion.

- Ask for their advice on something related to your business.

- Tell them they look nice.

- Give them a surprise just for doing business with you.

You can probably think of several more ways to make people feel important. The key is to do this in a natural manner so that each individual customer feels and believes you are taking a special and sincere interest in him or her.

You can recognize and reward your customers in other ways. Invite your customers to special sales or give them special treatment. Hold a contest for your best customers and give the winner a trip as a grand prize. Give other winners gift certificates or dinners at fine restaurants. Print up VIP cards for your best customers that entitle them to extra discounts.

All these ideas are strictly customer retention ideas—they have nothing to do with serving the customer during the time of a purchase. Yet they are vitally important to the success of your business because they create added value for the customer.

It is very easy for a competitor to price merchandise the same as you do, to give the same type of guarantees as you do, and to provide the same extensive and courteous service as you do. If that happens, the only thing that will make a customer choose to do business with you is the value-added service you provide.

The chart on the following page will help you create your own customer recognition and reward program. Use the first column to describe the customer's action, the second to show that you recognize that behavior of the customer, the third to explain how you will reward that behavior. Remember, it is better to create a shorter list and do those things extremely well than to try to do many things adequately.

RECOGNITION AND REWARD PROGRAM (continued)

Customer Action	How Recognized	How Rewarded
Samples:		
First Referral	Thank you note	Small discount
Second Referral	Telephone call	Box of candy
High Volume purchase	Telephone call	Dinner

Employee Recognition And Reward Programs

Any customer retention program must include recognition and rewards for your employees. Remember that they are your customers, too, and on some occasions, they are your most important customers. Show them you care about them as much as you do about the external customers. Create a recognition and reward program for your employees just as you did for your customers in the last section.

When you treat employees as customers, their morale will improve, and they will want to do well for the company. Furthermore, they will want to continue working for you. Customers like to see the same faces all the time. Both your customers and your employees will enjoy the stability. People like doing business with people they know and like. Long-term employees provide that for you with your customers. Therefore, never forget or neglect your employees. Always treat them as customers. It is as important to retain them as it is to retain your external customers.

7. CUSTOMER SPECIAL EVENTS

Special events for your special customers are a great way to strengthen the relationship. Many companies have special sales for the general public while others have private sales for their credit card holders. You, too, can create a special event for your best customers.

Host a cocktail party or other social gathering at your place of business after hours. Invite several good customers to dinner at a nice restaurant. Treat them to a round of golf, tickets to a sporting event or show, or do something special for their families.

Special events for special people do not have to be elaborate or expensive. They only have to be special. Ask your customers what is important and special to them. Then, wait a short while and give them what they want and like. They will reward you with their loyalty.

8. STRATEGIC ALLIANCES AND PARTNERSHIPS

You would keep more of your customers if you made more of them your partners. This is not as crazy an idea as it may seem at first. You do not have to make your customers financial partners in your business. Rather, you make them partners in doing business. Here are a few suggestions.

SITE VISITS

Invite your customers to spend a day with you at your place of business. Let them go anywhere they please, ask questions of anyone, and even try to work for a while. Ask them to view everything with a critical eye.

Having them on site can be of tremendous benefit to you. First, it shows them you care enough to invite them into your business. Second, it tells them you think they are important, because you are asking their opinion on how to improve your business. Third, it helps you get an objective opinion from an outsider on how well your business is running.

After you invite customers on site, the next step in creating the strategic partnership is for you to visit your customers. This may be at their place of business, at their homes (depending on how close you have become with them) or at a social function. If you want to make a customer a strategic partner, you must become intimately involved with them. You must also offer to help them, just as they are helping you.

This idea of strategic partners may not be as new to you as you may think. Don't you work with one accountant? Do you have a personal physician? How many financial planners or stock brokers are you working with? How many suppliers are you working with? How long have you been working with these people?

All these relationships are strategic partnerships. You are helping these people succeed just as they are helping you succeed. Why shouldn't you do the same thing with your customers? Remember that it is easier and less expensive to do business with a current customer than to acquire a new one. And you will have more current customers if you create more strategic partnerships.

CUSTOMER AS SALES AGENT

Customers who perceive themselves as strategic partners for your business become your best sales agents. They will tell others about how great it is to do business with you. These new customers will come to you with a positive attitude because you have already been endorsed by someone they trust. It is up to you not to let the new customers down.

On the other hand, customers who are not your strategic partners may not say anything good about you. They may not say anything bad, but they also may not say anything. No reference means no sale for you.

Therefore, try to make every customer a strategic partner. They can help you more than you know. And, even if there is someone who does not become your customer today, plant the seed for a strategic partnership in the future. You will be glad you did.

RETENTION THROUGH RECOVERY

Not all customers are happy customers. Sometimes you have to make up for bad service or a bad product. Service recovery means actions that tell the customer you will take care of their problem. Restitution is what you give your customers to compensate them for their inconvenience. You should welcome any situation that requires service recovery and restitution.

Most recovery and restitution opportunities result from customer complaints. These complaints do not have to be loud or demanding. They can be very quiet and, sometimes, almost go unnoticed. Yet, if you reread the Startling Service Statistics concerning the number of people who don't complain compared to those who do, you will find that you should welcome complaints as a part of doing business. If someone complains, they are taking the time to help you improve your business. You, then, must take the time to acknowledge and resolve their complaints.

Every business or organization will have to face the fact that sometime, some customer will be unhappy, dissatisfied or upset with their product or service. It is your responsibility to resolve the problem as quickly as possible to the customer's satisfaction.

You probably already have some type of recovery and restitution program in place. Use the chart below to outline your program. Fill in the spaces in each column. Then read on to see if your program does all it could do.

Policy	Procedure	Exceptions (?)	Recovery/ Restitution
Returns	30 days w/ receipt	(Fill in here)	Exchange Product

SATISFYING UNHAPPY CUSTOMERS

Customers who complain feel annoyed, cheated or victimized. They also feel that their situation is the most important in the world. Understand these feelings and treat your customers accordingly. Dissatisfied customers tell up to 20 friends that they are unhappy with the way you do business. However, if you resolve their problems, 50%–74% of these same customers will do business with you again. Adapt the following five-step recovery program to your business and specific situation, and then train your employees to be sure it's implemented.

SERVICE RECOVERY PROGRAM

1. **Apologize.**
   First and foremost, say you are sorry for the inconvenience the customer has experienced. Be sincere—the customer will notice if you are not. A sincere apology usually defuses the customer's anger. Also, you must personally accept responsibility for the problem occurring and its resolution.

2. **Urgent restatement.**
   Restate the problem as the customer described it to you to make certain you understand exactly what the customer means. Then, tell (and show, if possible) the customer that you will do everything possible to solve the problem and resolve the complaint immediately. Even if you can't resolve the problem to their fullest satisfaction, the customer will perceive that you were sincere and definitely intended to help. Their dissatisfaction will diminish.

3. **Empathy.**
   Make certain you communicate clearly to your customers so that they understand that you know how they feel. Do not patronize or try to pacify them. Just show them and tell them you understand how they feel. Use phrases such as: ''I understand . . .,'' ''I know how you feel . . .,'' ''I can see why you're upset.''

SATISFYING UNHAPPY CUSTOMERS
(continued)

4. **Restitution.**

Here is your chance to make points. Not only will you take immediate action to resolve your customers' complaints, such as refunding their money, making an exchange or offering a credit, you will go a step further. Tell and show your customers you will make it up to them in some special way. You may have to provide them with a free gift for their troubles, or you may have to allow them to purchase a new item at a sale price. Whatever you do, look at it as adding value rather than spending extra money.

5. **Follow up.**

This is where most programs fail. Be sure to find out if your customer is satisfied. You can ask a simple question or two at the end of the recovery process: "Have we resolved your complaint to your satisfaction? What else may we do for you?" Then wait a few days and call the customer to make certain they are still satisfied. You can also send them a letter. A nice touch would be to enclose a coupon or gift certificate with the letter. Going the extra mile will help you create and keep a loyal customer. Also, keep track of what you did and said as well as how the customer responded. This will help you the next time the customer does business with you.

Use this basic five-step approach to service recovery and restitution as a guide to develop a workable program for your business. You may want to break the restitution step down into resolution (the action taken to resolve the complaint) and restitution (anything else that you do for the customer to compensate them for their inconvenience). Whatever you do, this program will also help you to consider service recovery and restitution as part of a larger complaint management program.

MANAGING COMPLAINTS FOR CUSTOMER RETENTION

This basic approach for handling a complaint and keeping a customer is also a unique sales opportunity. A customer is more motivated to buy from you right at the time you have taken special care of them (resolved their complaint) than at any other time. Once you have resolved the complaint to their satisfaction, you can begin working on a new sale. Use the 10 suggestions on turning customer complaints into additional sales to create loyal and long-term customers for your business.

TURN CUSTOMER COMPLAINTS INTO SALES

1. Understand why the customer is complaining. Most probably, a need has not been satisfied or an expectation has not been met.

2. Listen attentively. The customer wants your undivided attention and respect concerning this problem, and he or she deserves to get it.

3. Handle one complaint at a time, even if the customer has several. You can manage a single complaint most effectively and have a better chance of turning that complaint into a sale than trying to handle two or three complaints at once.

4. Ask the customer what the needs were at the time of purchase and why those needs are not now being met. Find out how the current needs differ from the original, and why the change occurred.

5. Tell the customer that you understand the complaint and that you are sorry there is a problem. Assure the customer that you will do everything possible to resolve the complaint immediately.

6. Once you have resolved the complaint, discuss new sales offers and their benefits.

7. Handle any objections you may receive to the new sales offer, and continue to manage the original complaint if it comes up again.

8. Attempt to close the new sale resulting from the customer complaint as if it were an original sale. Sometimes, these ''complaint sales'' are easier because the customer has already made a purchase and knows how your product or service can satisfy a need.

9. If you cannot resolve the complaint to the customer's satisfaction, offer alternatives such as speaking to a person of higher authority, exchanging the merchandise, or refunding their money.

10. More than 75% of the people who complain and have that complaint resolved immediately will make another purchase. Use this statistic to your advantage as you continue to try to close the ''complaining'' customer.

HOW TO C.A.R.E. FOR YOUR CUSTOMERS

When resolving a service or performance problem, you must show the customers you CARE about them. If you CARE, your customers will reward you with their loyalty. To CARE properly for your customers, you must be:

Credible. Credibility, or your reputation, is really all you have in the business world. Customers must believe in your product or service, your customer service policies and procedures, your performance efforts and those of your staff. If they don't believe in you, they will not buy from you. Customers buy only for four reasons: to save or make money, to save time, to feel secure (have peace of mind) or to boost their egos. If you promise that your product or service will do one or more of these four things for your customers, then it better perform. If it doesn't, you must implement your service recovery program to ensure their satisfaction and loyalty.

Accessible. Customers want to be able to access your customer service system quickly and easily. They are already upset about something. Don't make it more difficult for them by passing them from employee to employee. Be accessible and customer friendly.

Reliable. Customers want to know what to expect from your business. You must do what you say you will do at the time you say you will do it. You must get it right the first time, get it done for the customer on time, and then check with the customer to ensure satisfaction. Reliability comes from the consistency in the performance of your product or service and the consistency with which you treat customers. When you are reliable, customers know what to expect from you and they feel comfortable doing business with you.

Excellence. Don't accept anything less. You and your employees must strive for excellence all the time. Customers believe that they themselves are important and excellent, and they want to do business with excellent companies and people. Provide excellent customer service and you will have excellent customer retention. Provide excellent training programs for your staff and you will have excellent performers who will ensure retention of your customers. If your work isn't excellent, it isn't good enough. Your customers want excellence and so should you.

Retaining your customers must become part of your regular business life. Follow the five basic steps for recovery and restitution, manage complaints so that you can turn them into additional sales, and CARE for the customer. If you do so, you will keep your customers for a long time.

RETENTION THROUGH TRAINING

Untrained employees present a bad image for your company. If your workers understand your product or service but cannot speak and listen to customers, you will not be in business very long. If your customers don't get the attention they deserve, they will take their business elsewhere.

Employee training is frequently an underutilized and underdeveloped method of customer retention. Most companies train their employees how to do their jobs but not how to interact wtih customers. Both are equally important.

Recent statistics estimate that if a company spends 2%–5% of its annual payroll on employee training, it should realize about a 10% increase in net profit. Futhermore, companies with superior customer service and a loyal customer base can charge up to 10% more than their competitors. So if you train your employees to provide superior customer service, your net profit can increase by 20%.

TYPES OF TRAINING PROGRAMS

You can provide many types of training programs for your employees. The most important programs for customer retention are:

- Customer service: company policies, systems and procedures

- Team building: developing cohesive and self-directed teams

- Communication skills (includes effective listening)

- Sales training basics (everybody sells)

These four programs are not that difficult to implement. If your company does not have the resources to develop these programs, outside consultants can provide training in these areas. To find these consultants, contact your local chapter of the American Society for Training and Development (ASTD) or your local colleges and junior colleges. One of these organizations will be able to direct you to qualified trainers who can help you develop and implement employee training programs in conjunction with your customer service and retention program.

If you decide to work with an outside consultant or trainer to upgrade the skills of your employees, you will probably go through the same process that others go through when they decide to do business with you. People choose to do business with someone for reasons such as convenience, price, location, or personal referral. Remember that when people choose you, they are your customers, and when you choose a trainer for your company, you are that trainer's customer.

The evaluation criteria questionnaire that follows represents the processes people go through when selecting a consultant or a business provider. Answer these questions accurately. They will help you select the person or training firm you need.

EVALUATION CRITERIA QUESTIONNAIRE

1. Does the consultant (business) demonstrate complete understanding of my problem, situation or needs?

2. Has the consultant (business) fully and accurately explained the approach (product or service) that will solve my problem?

3. Do I think the proposed approach will be successful?

4. What resources are available to make me a satisfied customer?

5. Is the consultant (business) qualified to provide me with the products and services I need?

6. Is the behavioral, communication and service style of the consultant (business) compatible with my own?

7. Will my problem be solved, or will my needs be met quickly?

8. Is the consultant (business) experienced enough for my situation?

9. Is the cost of the product or service fair, and am I getting good value for my money?

10. Do the references of the consultant (business) confirm the level and quality of service that I will be receiving?

Use these questions as a guide when selecting a trainer to develop the skills of your employees. Choose your consultant carefully. Remember—when you train your employees, they will perceive that you truly care about them. Not only will they provide superior service to your customers, they will also provide you with superior performance, productivity and loyalty. When you train your staff well, you, your business, your employees, your customers—everyone—wins.

RETENTION THROUGH RAPPORT AND EFFECTIVE COMMUNICATION

Every time you interact with a customer it is a moment of truth. It is a chance for you or your employees to represent the company positively and to satisfy a customer. These interactions will succeed or fail depending on how well rapport is established and how effectively you communicate with the customer. The skills for building rapport and strengthening communication are easily learned.

When a customer comes to you to make or exchange a purchase, request information or register a complaint, that customer wants to be heard. You must be an active and attentive listener so you can understand how the customer perceives the current situation, even though you may perceive it differently.

You and your customer each interpret any given situation based on your behavioral style and sensory perceptual style. We are all a combination of four behavioral styles: dominant, expressive, solid or analytical. Certain characteristics make up each type, which are shown in the Personality Factors chart on the next page.

You must know how to respond to your customers based on their particular behavioral styles. For example, a dominant customer is impatient and wants to control the situation to ensure he or she gets the desired results. Analytical types will be very precise and compliant with your rules for customer service and can be extremely persistent with their questioning. The Service Situation Planner on page 51 will help you respond to each behavioral type.

If you can respond appropriately to each behavioral type, you will develop rapport with that person. You can increase this rapport by "pacing" your customer. Pacing means that you mirror their body language, rate of speech, vocal tones and even eye movements.

Try to use the same words, phrases, slogans and slang your customers use, because their words will tell you their sensory perceptual style: visual, auditory or kinesthetic. A visual person speaks in pictures, images and sights. An auditory person talks about sounds, hearing and harmony. A kinesthetic person describes a situation in terms of feelings, senses and touch.

RAPPORT AND EFFECTIVE COMMUNICATION (continued)

BEHAVIORAL STYLES: PERSONALITY FACTORS

DOMINANT

- Goal oriented/results oriented
- Impatient
- Task oriented/high achiever
- Workaholic
- Decisive
- Opinionated/stubborn/blunt
- Innovative
- Tough/firm in relationships
- Control oriented
- Competitive/loves challenges

EXPRESSIVE

- Dreamer
- Unrealistic goals
- Creative; ideas flow
- Needs approval and compliments
- Generalizes
- Persuasive, outgoing
- Opinionated
- Fast decisions
- Excitable
- Enthusiastic, shows confidence

SOLID

- Needs people
- Good listener
- Status quo/dislikes change
- No risks
- No pressure
- Counselor/helps others
- Questioning
- Insecure/needs reassurance
- Supportive
- No conflict

ANALYTICAL

- Planner/organizer
- Details/technicalities
- Slow decisions
- Must be right
- Conservative/cautious
- Low pressure
- Precise/critical/logical
- Problem solver
- Persistent
- Follows procedures/compliant

BEHAVIORAL STYLES: SERVICE SITUATION PLANNER

"D" DOMINANT	"E" EXPRESSIVE
Be clear, specific, brief and efficient.	Plan interaction that supports their feelings/intuitions. Be stimulating. Use enough time to be sociable, yet fast-moving.
Stick to business.	
Present the facts logically.	Leave time for relating, socializing after completing service encounter.
Ask specific (preferably "what") questions.	
Provide service choices.	Talk about people, their goals, opinions they find stimulating.
Provide facts and figures about the results of your service.	Don't discuss extensive details related to service.
If you disagree, take issue with facts, not the person.	Ask for their opinions/ideas regarding how to service them better.
Motivate and persuade by referring to objectives and results.	Provide ideas for implementing action.
Support, maintain, use discretion.	Provide testimonials from people they perceive as important, prominent.
	Offer special, immediate and extra incentives for their willingness to accept your service offer.
	Continue supporting the relationship, be casual.
	Recognize their accomplishments.

"S" SOLID	"A" ANALYTICAL
Start (briefly) with a personal commitment. Be agreeable.	Approach them in a straightforward, direct but low keyed way; stick to business.
Show sincere interest in them as people.	Support their logical, methodical approach; build your credibility by listing pros and cons of your service approach.
Listen well. Be responsive and supportive.	
Elicit personal goals and work to help achieve these goals as related to service.	Present specifics and do what you say you can do. Take your time, but be persistent.
Ask "how" questions.	Create a schedule to implement service actions with step-by-step timetable. Assure them there won't be surprises.
If you agree easily, look for possible areas of their disagreement or dissatisfaction.	
If you disagree, look for hurt feelings.	If you agree, follow through and document for the record.
Be informal, orderly and friendly.	If you disagree, make an organized presentation of your position and ask for their suggestions to resolve the situation.
Guarantee their decision will minimize risks.	
Offer clear, specific solutions with guarantees.	Give them time to verify predictability of your actions; be accurate, realistic.
	Provide solid, tangible, practical evidence and options for future service performance.
	Provide long-term guarantees.

RAPPORT AND EFFECTIVE COMMUNICATION (continued)

Rapport and effective communication is enhanced when you use the same types of words your customer uses. If your customer says, "It sounds to me like this product is not working properly," do not respond, "I see what you are saying." You answer, "I hear what you are saying. What sound tells you the product is not working properly?"

When you establish good rapport and communication with your customers, they will want to continue doing business with you and will refer others to you. The result is more business and more customers staying with you for a longer period of time.

When your customers say they enjoy doing business with you because you are so much like them, you understand them, you know almost exactly what they are thinking and you provide excellent service, you have received one of the greatest compliments any businessperson can.

SENSORY PERCEPTUAL STYLE PROCESSOR EQUIVALENTS

Every sensory perceptual style has its own language by which it processes information. The language of one style has an equivalent in the other two styles. These are called processor equivalents. It is up to you, and necessary for your complete understanding of sensory perceptual styles, to identify these and other terms related to each particular style. For example, anything having to do with seeing or images is visual, hearing or sounds or speaking is auditory, and feeling or touch is kinesthetic. The list below provides you with some of these processor equivalents. Once you identify that the words someone uses belong to a specific sensory perceptual style, you must match those words and style to achieve rapport. This may mean you have to change your sensory perceptual communication style for a particular situation, because you want to communicate successfully.

VISUAL	AUDITORY	KINESTHETIC
See	Hear	Feel
Look	Listen	Touch
Bright	Loud	Pressing
Picture	Sound	Feeling
Colorful	Melodious	Exciting
Illuminate	Be heard	Be felt
Clear	Harmonious	Fits
Dawn	Tune in	Firm
Flash	Crescendo	Spike
Appear	Discuss	Aware
Perspective	Expression	Hands-on
Focused	Listen to	Secure
Foggy	Off-key	Clumsy
Strobe	Harsh	Irritate
Form	Resonance	Angle
Visual	Vocal	Do/act
Imagine	Speak	Be
Perception	Attention	Action
Blank out	Inner voices	Fidget

P A R T

III

50 Ways to
Keep Your Customers

50 WAYS TO KEEP YOUR CUSTOMERS FOR LIFE

You're almost there. So far, we've talked about customer service and going beyond customer service. Now here's a list of 50 things you can do to secure, satisfy, and retain your customers for life.

1. CREATE A SERVICE-ORIENTED CULTURE.

Everyone in the company must be customer-service oriented. All employees must realize that they work for the customer, and their job is to ensure the ultimate satisfaction of the customer. Everything else is superfluous.

2. HAVE A SERVICE VISION.

A vision is vital to the service success of any organization. A vision is more than just a philosophy of doing business. The vision must be the corporate cultural ethic. Everyone must believe and live the vision for your company to provide excellent customer service and keep customers for life. Management may develop the vision, but the staff must make it a reality.

3. TOTAL SUPPORT.

True success comes from total organizational support. It may be top management who decides to embark on a customer service program, but it is the line employees who implement the program. If these people don't support the initiative, the program won't work. Total support is needed.

4. POLICIES IN WRITING.

To benefit both your customers and your employees, put your service policies in writing. This way, there can be no mistakes or misunderstandings. Be aware, however, that your employees should have the authority to grant discretionary exceptions to the policies when the need arises. Remember, policies are guidelines, and they must remain flexible.

50 WAYS TO KEEP YOUR CUSTOMERS FOR LIFE (continued)

5. EMPLOYEE EMPOWERMENT.

Give your employees the authority to go with their responsibility of satisfying and keeping the customer. Allow them to make decisions on the spot and support those decisions. Remember, their job is to satisfy the customers and keep them coming back. Employees should not have to look for you or a manager every time a customer needs something out of the ordinary.

6. EMPLOYEE TRAINING.

Train, train and then retrain to retain your employees. Give them on-the-job training, off-the-job training, tapes, books, seminars, workshops, anything that will help them do their jobs better. While you may find qualified people who have just graduated from school, nothing prepares a person better for handling customers than the training they receive on the job and in practically applied programs.

7. MARKETING THE SERVICE PROGRAM.

All of your marketing should communicate that you provide superior customer service, are interested only in total customer satisfaction, and will do everything possible to keep your customers. This message must be stated in everything you send out to the public and the trades.

8. HIRE GOOD PEOPLE.

Hire people who are good and well qualified. Innate people skills go a long way toward helping your staff provide superior customer service and retain your customers.

9. DON'T MAKE CUSTOMERS PAY FOR SERVICE.

Pay for anything related to customer service, including shipping charges on returns, long distance telephone calls, postage, and anything else the customer is normally charged. If you don't pay for the cost of service, your competition will, and then your customers will become their customers.

10. REWARD LOYALTY.

What gets rewarded gets done. If you reward both customers and employees for their loyalty, they both will stay with you a long time. The rewards must be perceived as valuable by the recipient, but they do not have to cost you much money.

11. INSPECT WHAT YOU EXPECT.

What gets measured gets done. Measure the performance of your staff members and you will see an increase in performance levels, quality and productivity. You will also ultimately see an increase in profitability.

12. SET STANDARDS OF PERFORMANCE.

Let everyone know exactly what they must do to provide superior customer service. Make these standards as objective and measurable as possible, even though you may provide an intangible service. When people achieve these performance levels, customer retention and loyalty naturally follow.

13. TRADE JOBS.

Have your employees work in other departments. They will develop an appreciation for what other people in the company do, and therefore no employee will blame another for a customer problem. In fact, since the employees have experience in other areas, they will be able to solve more problems and satisfy more customers on the spot.

14. CROSS TRAIN.

Train your employees in other people's jobs. They will be able to provide more assistance to customers, more assistance to each other, and you will become less dependent on "irreplaceable" employees when they are not at work.

15. EASILY ACCESSIBLE SERVICE SYSTEMS.

Make your customer service systems easy for the customer to access. Have them reach a person on the telephone as soon as they call in, or have them speak with an employee who can help them as soon as they arrive at your place of business. Don't make it hard for customers to come to you. They may decide not to do business with you again.

50 WAYS TO KEEP YOUR CUSTOMERS FOR LIFE (continued)

16. USER FRIENDLY SERVICE SYSTEMS.

Make your customer service systems easy to use. The customer is the reason for your business, not someone who is in the way of doing business. Make the customers feel and know they can bring a problem to your attention, voice a complaint, get it resolved as quickly as possible and receive superb treatment during all their contacts with your company.

17. DESIGN FLEXIBILITY INTO YOUR SERVICE POLICIES.

Keep your policies flexible, because each customer and situation is different. Your employees must know they can modify a written or stated policy to ensure the customer's total satisfaction at any given moment, and you *must* support your employees' decisions and actions in these situations.

18. EDUCATE THE CUSTOMER.

Do not assume the customer knows what you know. Use every customer contact as a chance to educate the customer about something related to your business. Even if you are just educating them about your great return policy, teach them. They will be appreciative and show this by continuing to do business with you.

19. HANDLE COMPLAINTS PROPERLY.

Acknowledge that the customer is upset, listen carefully, assure them you are doing everything possible at this moment to resolve their complaint, and then resolve the complaint. Then, when they express appreciation for your efforts, use the opportunity to increase their loyalty. Thank them for bringing the problem to your attention, apologize again for the problem, and try to sell them something else.

20. TURN COMPLAINTS INTO ADDITIONAL SALES.

The customer is most receptive to continuing to do business with you after you resolve a complaint. Using this opportunity to make a sale is both ethical and practical. Your customers will appreciate your interest in them. They will probably buy from you now and go out and tell their friends how well and quickly you handled their problem. You will develop a reputation with customers of credibility, reliability and honesty.

21. TRAIN YOUR EMPLOYEES TO DO IT RIGHT THE FIRST TIME.
Repair, rework and additional free services are very costly. Doing it right the first time guarantees greater profitability, happier customers and more long-term customers. If you must do something over again for a customer, do it even "righter" the second time.

22. EVERY CUSTOMER HAS A LIFETIME VALUE.
When a customer buys from you, that purchase is not a one time, one price deal. Consider the potential that customer brings to your business. How much money could that customer spend with you over a lifetime? That amount is the lifetime value of a customer and that is the type and level of service they should receive every time they do business with you.

23. BEG FOR CUSTOMER FEEDBACK.
It is not enough to send out surveys or leave comment cards at the cash register. You must get as much customer feedback as possible, even if you have to beg for it. If customers are asked their opinion and see that you have implemented their suggestions, they will not only continue to do business with you, they will recommend that friends come to you also. Do whatever you can to solicit their opinions and comments, and then act on their suggestions.

24. IDENTIFY CUSTOMER VALUES, BELIEFS AND STANDARDS.
Your service programs must be geared to the values, beliefs, and standards of your customers. If customer values and your values conflict, invite your customers into the business for a discussion to find out why the difference exists and what can be done about it. Then decide if you must modify your position to maintain customer satisfaction and loyalty. However, you should never compromise your ethics and values to satisfy a customer.

50 WAYS TO KEEP YOUR CUSTOMERS FOR LIFE (continued)

25. GET AND USE EMPLOYEE IDEAS.

Your employees who have daily contact with customers know more about what customers need, want and expect than you or any other manager could ever hope to know. Get feedback from your employees, listen carefully to their suggestions, and implement as many as possible. Research shows that the best service companies not only get more ideas from their employees, they use more of them. This makes employees feel wanted and cared about and shows them that you think as much of your internal customers as you do your external customers.

26. BE FAIR AND CONSISTENT.

Customers may not always like or agree with what you do for them, but as long as you treat each one fairly and consistently, they will respect you for it. Consistency enhances your credibility and reliability which are essential for building loyalty and retaining customers.

27. UNDERPROMISE AND OVERDELIVER.

Customers' expectations can be unrealistically raised when businesses overpromise and underdeliver. Usually, the business cannot meet these expectations, and the customer goes away disappointed. But if you set realistic expectations for the customer on your quality and level of service and then exceed those expectations, the customer is more than satisfied. Remember, though, that you should not underpromise to the extent that you insult your customers. They will see through you in a minute and take their business elsewhere.

28. COMPETE ON BENEFITS, NOT PRODUCTS OR PRICES.

Customers can always find another product at a lower price, somehow, somewhere. You must always remind your customers of the benefits of doing business with you. Features can be found in every product, but benefits are unique to the way you do business.

29. HIGH TOUCH IS MORE IMPORTANT THAN HIGH TECH.
High tech does get people to say "WOW!", but it doesn't get people to care about other people. Your business needs high touch to survive. Stay close to your customers. Get to know them well. The closer you are to your customers, the longer they will do business with you. After all, when you show you care, you become like one of the family.

30. ASK CUSTOMERS WHAT THEY WANT.
Constantly ask your customers what they want from you, what you can do for them and how you can do it better. They may want a new product or service, extended hours or just something minor that will make them happier. You will never know unless you ask. After you ask, you must give them what they want. They will reward your generosity with loyalty.

31. DAILY SERVICE MANAGEMENT.
Every employee in every department is involved in providing superior service to achieve the ultimate goal—keeping the customer for life. Do everything possible to make everyone's job easier so that it will be easier for them to give the customers what they want. If there is a problem during the day, make the necessary adjustments and resolve it quickly.

32. KNOW THE COST OF LOSING A CUSTOMER.
All employees should know the lifetime value of a customer, the cost of losing even one, and the effect that loss can have on your business. Consider rewarding your employees if they retain your customers over a longer-than-average time period.

50 WAYS TO KEEP YOUR CUSTOMERS
FOR LIFE (continued)

33. KNOW YOUR COMPETITION.

What kinds of customer services are your competitors providing? What are they doing to retain their customers? Are they offering more benefits, better service policies, or are they just being nicer to the customers? Find out, and if they are doing something you are not doing, then do it. If it works for them, it will probably work for you.

34. CONDUCT MARKET RESEARCH.

You can never have enough information about your customers. Do surveys, interviews, whatever it takes to find out what the marketplace wants. Then adapt your business accordingly. Information is not power unless you know how to use it.

35. CONDUCT INTERNAL ASSESSMENTS.

Constantly evaluate your company's customer service, satisfaction and retention. Interview your employees, have them fill out questionnaires, ask your customers at the point of purchase how you are doing, and then use this information to improve your service and retention efforts. Examples of simple surveys for you to use are provided in Appendix II.

36. KNOW WHAT YOUR CUSTOMERS NEED, WANT, AND EXPECT.

Businesses run into problems when they think customers need, want or expect one thing when they really require another. These gaps in perceptions about service delivery ultimately disappoint customers. Find out what the customers need, want and expect, and then give it to them.

37. FIND, NURTURE AND DISPLAY CUSTOMER CHAMPIONS.

Every business has one, two or several employees who are true customer champions. Find out who these people are, nurture and support them, then make them role models for everyone else to follow. Reward their behavior. The rest of your staff will upgrade their service performance to this level to receive similar rewards. The result is a highly motivated, service-oriented staff and a group of satisfied and loyal customers.

38. EFFECTIVE COMMUNICATION IS CRITICAL TO SUCCESS.

Every problem between people is the result of poor communication. Train your people to develop effective communication skills: how to listen first, how to speak so others will listen, how to understand others before trying to be understood, how to receive and give feedback, and how to develop rapport with customers.

39. RAPPORT IS THE KEY TO SUCCESSFUL COMMUNICATION.

The technical skills of communication can be acquired and used, but without rapport there is no communication. The skills of developing rapport can be taught and your employees should learn them. When employees and customers have rapport, there is a feeling of trust and a desire to continue to do business.

40. SMILE.

Smiling is important when serving a customer. Smiles will usually get a smile in return, but smiles will not guarantee quality customer service. Smiling must be something employees do because it makes them feel good, and it makes the customers feel good.

41. MAKE CUSTOMERS FEEL IMPORTANT.

The more important you make customers feel, the better they will feel about doing business with you. Call them by name, ask them to tell you about themselves and ask questions about their accomplishments. Your reward will be a lifetime customer.

42. PROMOTE YOUR CUSTOMERS.

With their permission, of course, use your customers in your marketing and promotion efforts. Let them tell their story to other customers and prospects. This third party endorsement fosters tremendous credibility, and your customers will love being involved.

50 WAYS TO KEEP YOUR CUSTOMERS FOR LIFE (continued)

43. CREATE A CUSTOMER COUNCIL.

Your customer council, like a board of directors or focus group, should meet regularly to scrutinize your business and the service you provide. The council makes suggestions on which you act.

44. MARKET FREQUENT BUYER PROGRAMS.

To get your customers excited about doing business with you, start a reward program for frequent buyers. You can use coupons, punch cards or anything else that helps you keep track of customer activity. When purchases reach a certain level, reward your customers with a gift—a deep discount coupon, a free product or service or something more expensive, such as a trip.

45. ACCEPT ONLY EXCELLENCE.

If you expect average performance and service, that is what you will get. Therefore, set your expectations high. Accept only excellent performance from your employees, and train your staff to achieve these levels of performance. Good enough should never be good enough.

46. EMPLOYEES ARE CUSTOMERS, TOO.

Employees are your internal customers, your first line of customers, and each of them has a customer somewhere in the value chain. Each employee must provide excellent customer service to every other employee so that they all can provide superior service to customers. This is the only way to guarantee customer satisfaction and retention.

47. LET CUSTOMERS KNOW YOU CARE.

Send them thank you cards, holiday cards and anything else you can to show them you care. Never let them forget your name. Teach them that whenever they need something, they can come to you for it because you care. Spend time and money marketing your caring attitude to your customers.

48. MAKE SERVICE RESULTS VISIBLE.

Visibility enhances credibility, and credibility is only enhanced by improved performance. Post your customer comment cards and letters for all customers to see. Create a testimonial book for customers to read. Post employees' performance results in their lounge or locker room. Make service results visible so that your employees will constantly improve and your customers will be the beneficiaries of this improved service.

49. GO THE EXTRA MILE.

When customers want something from you, give it to them. Then do something extra. They will be grateful and you will have a long term customer.

50. MARKETING AND CUSTOMER SERVICE GO HAND IN HAND.

All of your marketing efforts should communicate your customer service message. In today's competitive marketplace, the only thing that differentiates companies is the level and quality of their customer service, and this is the major criteria people use to decide whether or not to continue purchasing from that company. Customer service is a very effective and powerful marketing tool, and marketing is a very effective and powerful customer service tool. Combined, the two will help you keep your customers for life.

50 WAYS TO KEEP YOUR CUSTOMERS FOR LIFE (continued)

Now, review everything you are doing and make it better.

Whatever you are doing now to service and satisfy your customers may not be sufficient to keep them tomorrow. A competitor will offer superior customer service on a better product at a lower price that has more benefits. You have to stay one step ahead of your competitors. You must know what they're doing and how they're doing it. Review your customer service policy, then do whatever it takes to make it better.

Remember, you are in business to make money, and the only way you will make money is to have satisfied customers who keep coming back.

A P P E N D I X

I

Customer Service
Tips and Lists

*Note: Some of the materials in the following lists has been compiled from a variety of sources, even if the specific sources or authors are not mentioned directly.

10 COMMANDMENTS OF SUPERIOR CUSTOMER SERVICE AND RETENTION

1. The customer is the most important person in the company.

2. The customer is not dependent on you—you are dependent on the customer. You work for the customer.

3. The customer is not an interruption of your work. The customer is the purpose of your work.

4. The customer does you a favor by visiting or calling your business. You are not doing the customer a favor by serving them.

5. The customer is as much a part of your business as anything else, including inventory, employees and your facility. If you sold the business, the customers would go with it.

6. The customer is not a cold statistic. The customer is a person with feelings and emotions, just like you. Treat the customer better than you would want to be treated.

7. The customer is not someone to argue with or match wits with.

8. It is your job to satisfy the needs, wants and expectations of your customers and, whenever possible, resolve their fears and complaints.

9. The customer deserves the most attentive, courteous and professional treatment you can provide.

10. The customer is the lifeblood of your business. Always remember that without customers, you would not have a business. You work for the customer.

TIPS FOR LONG-TERM CUSTOMER RETENTION

- Call each customer by name.

- Listen to what each customer has to say.

- Be concerned about each customer as an individual.

- Be courteous to each customer.

- Be responsive to the individual needs of each customer.

- Know your customers' personal buying histories and motivations.

- Take sufficient time with each customer.

- Involve customers in your business. Ask for their advice and suggestions.

- Make customers feel important. Pay them compliments.

- Listen first to understand the customer. Then speak so they can understand you.

CUSTOMER'S BILL OF RIGHTS

The customer has a right to the following:

1. Professional, courteous and prompt service

2. Your full and undivided attention each time the customer chooses to do business with you

3. Quality products and services

4. Fulfillment of needs in a manner consistent with reasonable service expectations

5. Competent, knowledgeable and well-trained staff

6. Attention to every detail every time they access your customer service system

7. The benefits of all your resources, teamwork and networks to provide superior, long-term service

8. Open channels of communication for feedback, complaints or compliments

9. A fair price for your products or services

10. Appreciation from you and your staff for past and future business

7 CHECKPOINTS TO SUCCESSFUL CUSTOMER RETENTION

 1. Have a clear customer service mission, vision and philosophy. Communicate this to your employees, then train and empower them to carry out your service mission.

 2. Provide customers with quality products, services and care.

 3. Listen closely to your customers, and then act on their suggestions. Do the same for your employees.

 4. Pay attention to your own intuition when serving customers, and have your employees pay attention to their own intuitions.

 5. Treat customers with respect, trust, fairness, honesty and integrity.

 6. Communicate with your customers regularly, including current customers, former customers and your competitor's customers.

 7. Expand your product and service offerings carefully, ensuring that you can continue to provide quality customer service while you grow.

10 GREATEST CUSTOMER SERVICE AND RETENTION TIPS OF ALL TIME

1. Unique Service Philosophy

Businesses need a unique service philosophy or mission statement, which should complement their overall business mission statements. The service philosophy should describe exactly how customers will be treated when they purchase products and services from you and your preferred outcomes for every service encounter.

2. Customer Feedback

Get customer feedback any way you can. Set up customer councils, focus groups, hand out surveys in your place of business, mail out surveys, conduct personal interviews, and beg your customers for feedback. The more you involve customers with your business, the more they will tell you how to improve it. Listen, evaluate the information, and act on the suggestions.

3. Service and Retention Programs

Use your customer service system and your customer retention program as powerful marketing tools. Call your customers, send them thank you and holiday cards, mail them newsletters. Do anything and everything you can to keep them informed about your business. The more they see your name, the greater the probability they will continue to do business with you.

4. Close the Gap

What customers expect from a business can be quite different from what they receive. The same holds true for what the business thinks customers want and what the customers actually want. Work to close these gaps so your perceptions of situations coincide with those of your customers.

5. Meet and Exceed Expectations

Customers have expectations they bring to every business situation. You must meet these expectations to satisfy the customer. You must exceed these expectations to ensure their long-term loyalty. Exceeding expectations is the key to retention and repurchase.

6. Customer Reward Programs

What gets rewarded gets done. Any type of reward program aimed at the customer, such as frequent buyer or referral programs, will motivate the customer to continue purchasing from you. Rewards make the customer feel special, and customers will return to the source of that special feeling. Do this for your employees also.

10 GREATEST CUSTOMER SERVICE AND RETENTION TIPS OF ALL TIME (continued)

7. Public Identity

The identity you create for your business must match the identity customers perceive of themselves. Identity is just one factor customers use in deciding to purchase from you. The image and identity you create in the community, backed up by your actions, influences when and how long customers buy from you.

8. Community Service

Community service, charity tie-ins and environmental issues have a large influence on customer expectations. Make sure your customers know of your efforts in these areas. Your community service will help them feel good about doing business with you.

9. Easily Accessible, User Friendly Service Systems

Make it extremely easy for customers to get service from you. When they need something, have it for them, including new products, returns, refunds, solutions to complaints or anything else they need. Keep your rules, regulations, policies and procedures flexible. They should be guidelines, not laws.

10. Train and Empower Your Employees

Quality employees provide quality service. Train your employees to do their jobs and provide superior customer service. Then give your employees the authority to make decisions to satisfy the customer, even if it goes against company policy. Support your employees in all their decisions to satisfy and keep the customer, because without customers there is no business.

One last thought!

Always remember that your employees are your first line of customers. These internal customers must be treated with the same care, respect and importance as your external (buying) customers. If you want your employees to provide superior service and work to keep the customers, you must provide superior service to your employees and work to keep them.

A P P E N D I X

II

Customer Service, Satisfaction and Retention Inventories

The importance of self-assessment and evaluation cannot be overemphasized. The following series of surveys will help you evaluate your customer service efforts, including how well you provide service, how well your staff provides service, and how satisfied your customers are with your service. The results of these surveys will indicate your customer service strengths and weaknesses. In all surveys, the higher the number the more favorable the response. Feel free to adapt the surveys to suit your particular needs.

CUSTOMER SERVICE
SELF-ASSESSMENT

Respond to each statement by placing the number that best describes your answer in the space provided. Use the following scale:

1	2	3	4	5
Never	Rarely	Sometimes	Usually	Often

_____ 1. I accept people without judging them.

_____ 2. I show patience, courtesy and respect to people regardless of their behavior toward me.

_____ 3. I maintain my composure and refuse to become irritated or frustrated when coping with an angry or irate person.

_____ 4. I treat people as I would want them to treat me.

_____ 5. I help others maintain their self-esteem, even when the situation requires negative or critical feedback.

_____ 6. I do not get defensive when interacting with another person, even if their comments are directed at me.

_____ 7. I realize that my attitude toward myself and others affects the way I respond in any given situation.

_____ 8. I realize that each person believes his or her problem is the most important and urgent thing in the world at this time, and I attempt to help them resolve it immediately.

_____ 9. I treat everyone in a positive manner, regardless of how they look, dress or speak.

_____ 10. I view every interaction with another person as a "golden moment," and I do everything in my power to make it a satisfactory and win-win situation for both of us.

SERVICE RATING SCALE

Using a scale of 1 to 10 with 10 being the best, please rate how well you and your staff provide each of the following services:

Service	Self	Staff
a. Prompt and courteous answering of the telephones	_____	_____
b. Accurate responses to telephone inquiries	_____	_____
c. Providing individualized and personalized attention to each client	_____	_____
d. Marketing and promoting the business to current and new clients	_____	_____
e. Marketing and promoting the business to professional and other referral sources	_____	_____
f. Communicating prices and billing procedures clearly and concisely	_____	_____
g. Providing high quality, courteous and friendly service to all clients	_____	_____
h. Requesting and quickly resolving customer complaints	_____	_____
i. Keeping clients informed and updated about current and new developments regarding the business	_____	_____
j. Tracking the effectiveness of marketing and service efforts	_____	_____

CUSTOMER SERVICE INVENTORY

We are interested in finding out what you think about our services. Please respond to each statement by placing the number of the appropriate response in the blank space next to the statement.

1	2	3	4	5
Never	*Once in a while*	*Half the time*	*Often*	*Very Often*

_____ **1.** The telephone is answered by the third ring.

_____ **2.** The person answering the telephone is courteous and friendly.

_____ **3.** I am placed on hold for more than 30 seconds.

_____ **4.** My call is directed to the appropriate person.

_____ **5.** The office (store) is conveniently located and easy to find.

_____ **6.** There is ample parking available near the office (store).

_____ **7.** The atmosphere of the office (store) is warm and inviting.

_____ **8.** The regularly scheduled office (store) hours are convenient for me.

_____ **9.** The salesperson or the service provider greets me immediately.

_____ **10.** I wait less than 15 minutes if my appointment is delayed.

_____ **11.** Prices are appropriate for the products and services provided.

_____ **12.** Payment terms for the products or services are flexible.

_____ **13.** Payment methods are acceptable.

_____ **14.** I receive good value for my money.

_____ **15.** The office (store) staff is courteous and friendly.

CUSTOMER SERVICE INVENTORY
(continued)

_____ **16.** The service provider and/or staff is courteous and friendly.

_____ **17.** I receive personalized attention and service.

_____ **18.** My complaints are resolved quickly and to my satisfaction.

_____ **19.** The service provider and/or staff answers all my questions to my satisfaction.

_____ **20.** The service provider and/or staff is concerned about my situation.

_____ **21.** I am involved in decisions regarding my purchase.

_____ **22.** I feel comfortable with the personality of the service provider (staff).

_____ **23.** I am kept informed of all details regarding my purchase.

_____ **24.** I am happy with the way the service provider (staff) treats me.

_____ **25.** I feel the service provider (staff) is qualified to provide me with these services.

_____ **26.** I prefer to use these services rather than those provided by someone else.

_____ **27.** I can schedule an appointment or shop at the store when it is convenient for me.

_____ **28.** I will use this service provider (store) again.

_____ **29.** I would refer people to this service provider (store).

_____ **30.** The overall quality of the service is high.

Thank you for completing this inventory. Your answers will help us to understand your needs and improve the quality of the services we offer to you.

CUSTOMER SATISFACTION SURVEY

We are interested in finding out how satisfied you are with the services and treatment you received. Please respond to each statement by placing the number of the appropriate response in the blank space next to the statement.

1	2	3	4	5
Extremely dissatisfied	*Slightly dissatisfied*	*Neither satisfied nor dissatisfied*	*Slightly satisfied*	*Extremely satisfied*

How satisfied are you with:

_____ 1. The location of the office (store)

_____ 2. The parking around the office (store)

_____ 3. The scheduled office (store) hours

_____ 4. The office (store) atmosphere and decor

_____ 5. The telephone manners of the staff

_____ 6. The treatment you receive from the staff

_____ 7. The treatment you receive from the service provider

_____ 8. The prices for the services

_____ 9. The payment methods and terms

_____ 10. The quality of the services

_____ 11. The qualifications of the service provider

_____ 12. The manner in which your complaints are handled

_____ 13. The manner in which your questions are answered

_____ 14. The professionalism of the staff

_____ 15. The marketing and advertising programs of the service provider

A P P E N D I X

III

Customer Information and Profile

The best way to satisfy and retain your customers is to know as much about them as possible. You should know their likes and dislikes, their buying histories, their needs and wants and anything else that will help you seem more personable to them. Your goal is always to maintain their loyalty and retain them as customers.

Most companies are now computerized, either at the point of purchase or in the back room. If you have a customer database, use it. It is your most effective service and marketing tool. If you do not have a computer for your business, the following two forms will help you.

Your customers may complete the classification information form or it can be filled out by your staff, who ask the customers the questions. The customer profile should be filled out by your staff so that all the necessary information is captured on the form. As always, you are free to adapt the forms to fit your business and specific situation.

CLASSIFICATION INFORMATION

To learn more about you and to continue providing you with high quality service, we would appreciate it if you would fill in the requested information. Thank you.

Name: _____

Address: _____

City: _____ _____ State: _____ Zip: _____

Telephone: (H) _____ (B) _____

Age: _____ Gender: M _____ F _____

Marital status: Married ____ Single ____ Divorced ____ Widowed ____

Family Size: _____ Occupation: _____

Education Completed: High School _____ Graduate School _____

College _____ Vocational/Trade _____

Date of Last Visit: _____

Household Income: (Check one)

$10,000 – $19,999 _____

$20,000 – $29,999 _____

$30,000 – $39,999 _____

$40,000 – $49,999 _____

$50,000 – $59,999 _____

$60,000 – $69,999 _____

$70,000 + _____

CUSTOMER PROFILE

Name: _____ Telephone: _____

Address: _____

City: _____ State: _____ Zip: _____

Personal Information:

Birthdate: _____ Anniversary: _____

Spouse's Name: _____ Children: _____

Characteristics/Likes/Dislikes: _____

_____

Special Interests/Hobbies: _____

Business Information:

Company Name: _____ Title: _____

Job Anniv.: _____ Telephone: _____

Secretary's Name: _____

Reports To: _____ Title: _____ Ext.: _____

Office Contacts: _____

Purchasing Authority: _____ Volume: _____

Purchase Habits/Preferences: _____

Currently Buys From: _____

Satisfaction Level: _____

Needs/Benefits/Solutions:

Current Needs: _____

Future Needs: _____

Current Problems: _____

Benefits/Solutions: _____

Call Date: _____ Response: _____

Next Call: _____ Action: _____

NOTES

NOTES

NOTES

NOTES

NOTES

NOTES

NOTES

OVER 150 BOOKS AND 35 VIDEOS AVAILABLE IN THE 50-MINUTE SERIES

We hope you enjoyed this book. If so, we have good news for you. This title is part of the best-selling *50-MINUTE™ Series* of books. All *Series* books are similar in size and identical in price. Many are supported with training videos.

To order *50-MINUTE* Books and Videos or request a free catalog, contact your local distributor or Crisp Publications, Inc., 1200 Hamilton Court, Menlo Park, CA 94025. Our toll-free number is (800) 442-7477.

50-Minute Series Books and Videos Subject Areas . . .

Management
Training
Human Resources
Customer Service and Sales Training
Communications
Small Business and Financial Planning
Creativity
Personal Development
Wellness
Adult Literacy and Learning
Career, Retirement and Life Planning

Other titles available from Crisp Publications in these categories

Crisp Computer Series
The Crisp Small Business & Entrepreneurship Series
Quick Read Series
Management
Personal Development
Retirement Planning